After You've Blown It

AFTER YOU'VE
BLOWN IT

LIFECHANGE BOOKS

ERWIN W. LUTZER

Multnomah® Publishers *Sisters, Oregon*

AFTER YOU'VE BLOWN IT
published by Multnomah Publishers, Inc.

© 2004 by Erwin Lutzer
International Standard Book Number: 1-59052-334-2

Cover image by Photonica/Giles A. Hancock

Unless otherwise indicated, Scripture quotations are from:
The Holy Bible, New International Version
© 1973, 1984 by International Bible Society,
used by permission of Zondervan Publishing House.
Other Scripture quotations are from:
The Holy Bible, New King James Version (NKJV)
© 1984 by Thomas Nelson, Inc.

Multnomah is a trademark of Multnomah Publishers, Inc.,
and is registered in the U.S. Patent and Trademark Office.
The colophon is a trademark of Multnomah Publishers, Inc.

Printed in the United States of America

For information:
MULTNOMAH PUBLISHERS, INC. • P. O. BOX 1720 • SISTERS, OR 97759

Library of Congress Cataloging-in-Publication Data

Lutzer, Erwin W.
  After you've blown it / by Erwin W. Lutzer.
      p. cm.
  ISBN 1-59052-334-2 (hard)
  1.   Christian life. 2.   Reconciliation—Religious aspects—Christianity.
I. Title.
  BV4501.3.L863 2004
  248.8'6—dc22

                                                                  2003022659

04 05 06 07 08 09 10—10 9 8 7 6 5 4 3 2 1 0

This message of hope is for my brothers and sisters
who need to be reminded that every saint
has a past and every sinner has a future.

*"But where sin increased,
grace increased all the more."*

Contents

WHO DESERVES REDEMPTION?

"Does Bob Greene deserve redemption?"

USA Today wanted to know. "Or should the renowned former columnist for the *Chicago Tribune* sit on the bench for the rest of his days, yoked by a scarlet letter?"[1]

Bob Greene first gained notoriety as a journalist writing powerful exposés about abandoned and abused children, sounding the alarm to parents and state officials. He wrote bestselling books and built a thirty-year career as a voice for those who had no say. By all accounts, Greene was a family man deeply committed to his wife and children.

Then an anonymous e-mail touched off a shocking scandal that exposed a pattern of philandering. Greene admitted to his indiscretions and was promptly fired by the *Tribune.* His wife died of a respiratory illness four months later.

Some say that Bob Greene deserves redemption. Others say he does not.

A fellow journalist said, "Greene is now a lost voice. I had never heard a man broken before—up close and personal." He marveled at how we gleefully pounce on people and leave them for dead. They are still people, after all.

Greene's response? "I was very good at my work, and I wasn't real good at my life." He added, "It's like I'm a body in the street and they keep coming by and kicking...but the body is already dead."

He now lives the life of a hermit, almost never venturing outside. And if he has a plan to come back, to revive his career, he has not revealed it.

Does Bob Greene deserve redemption?

If I could speak to Bob Greene today, I would say, "Yes, Bob, you deserve redemption." I would point out that he has two issues that need to be resolved. One is his fellowship with God. The other involves his relationships with others, particularly those whom he has hurt. His days as a journalist may indeed be over, but Greene still has a future in the eyes of God.

But what about the husband who, against his wife's urging, invested their savings in a risky enterprise that failed, forcing the family into bankruptcy? It looked like a deal the man couldn't refuse, but his wife insisted that the money should be put in a certificate of deposit. Now she won't let him forget that his foolishness has squandered their hard-earned savings, and so he lives under a cloud of criticism and deep personal regret.

This man deserves redemption.

What about the young unmarried woman who has had an abortion? She wanted to keep the child, but her parents urged her to terminate the pregnancy. She had shamed them, they said—their family had been well thought of in the local church. Fearful, weeping, and hesitant, the young woman pushed aside her own deep longings and did what she knew was wrong. She thought God might forgive her, but she doubted that her parents ever would. Now she feels like "damaged goods" unworthy of a decent man and unfit to serve the Lord.

This young woman deserves redemption.

So does the addict who called me to confess that he had accumulated thirty-five thousand dollars in credit card debt by gambling over the Internet. He told me that his wife had just discovered his well-guarded secret. What's more, this man was a teacher at a respected Christian college, and he feared that if the truth were to come out, he could be fired from his job.

Despite the mess he has made, this man also has a future with God.

Strictly speaking, of course, not one of us *deserves* redemption. God owes us nothing, but He nevertheless offers His undeserved grace. Though we deserve damnation, He invites each of us to be redeemed. Worthy or not, we come to Him to receive forgiveness and the assurance that God still has a plan for our lives.

We've all blown it. "All have sinned and fall short of the glory of God" (Romans 3:23).

I have said things I've later regretted. I felt as though I'd be better off having my mouth taped shut, and yet the words could not be recalled. I've failed those around me more times than I know, and I've often had to ask for forgiveness from those I love.

Whether we've blown it in a big way or through "small" indiscretions, we have all wished from the bottom of our hearts that we could relive some of our past days, this time getting it right. I'm reminded of the teenager who prayed, "God, I pray that this accident might never have happened." But the past is a brute fact that cannot be altered. All that can be changed is our response to it—the forgiveness we can receive from God and our attempts to reconcile with people we have hurt. We can still learn from our mistakes and hope for a better day.

This book is dedicated to all who have made unfortunate choices that later returned to haunt them. It's for all of us who need to be reminded that God is bigger than the mistakes we have made.

This is a book of hope.

A book for all of us who have ever made a wrong turn in the journey of life.

Chapter One

THE WAITING
FATHER

Every one of us has, at one time or another, made a wrong turn in the journey of life. Jesus once told a story about a young man who made a series of frightfully bad decisions. By his own admission, he did not deserve redemption. But after blowing it, he did do one thing right. The tale reminds us that as long as we are alive, there is still one good move we can make. The smart thing. The right thing.

You're probably familiar with the story. A father has two sons, the younger of whom has grown tired of working the farm, and so he comes to his father and asks for his inheritance. "Father, give me my share of the estate," he says

(Luke 15:12). And so the father divides his property between his two sons. The younger son then departs for a "distant country," where his father's money will underwrite his stay. Once there he takes his father's gifts and squanders them on an extravagant lifestyle.

Despite his fine upbringing, the boy is both impertinent and rude. By making this request of his father, he is saying, in effect, "Father, I can't wait for you to die, so give me my inheritance right now." The father does not argue. Nor does he lecture his son about the dangers of the wayward life, but instead chooses to let the youth follow his desires. There comes a time when a boy's decisions must be respected, even when they will lead to his ruin. And so the father hides his pain as he watches his son walk away down the long, perilous road.

The boy takes his inheritance and converts it into cash. He will need money the moment he arrives in the distant country. He believes that the good life, once begun, will last forever.

THE LONG AND NOT-SO-HAPPY ROAD

The young man's rebellion is deliberate.

First, he is intent on going to the "distant country." He knows that his father will not follow him, nor will his judgmental brother be able to seek him out. He goes where he is unknown, a place where he will not be chided for taking a wrong turn in the road. He opts for a life of independence without restraints.

Second, he spurns his father's values by enjoying those pleasures of which his father disapproved. Many of us are acquainted with the King James Version's description of the young man's life in the far country. We read that he "wasted his substance with riotous living" (v. 13). We use the same word today when we say, "He got wasted."

In the "distant country" we waste our minds. We waste our opportunities. We waste our money. When my wife and I attended a funeral of a high school student who over-dosed on drugs, I thought, *What a waste.* I once counseled a young woman who had become a single mother after a fling with a man she didn't care for. Now she was a high school dropout, and I thought, *What a waste.*

As for the young man in Jesus' story, his circumstances take a turn for the worse when famine comes to the land. It could be that the famine had already hit when he arrived, but he hadn't noticed it. When the money gives out, he is suddenly and painfully aware of the economic downturn.

Finally, the young man spurns his religion. He hires himself out to a citizen of this country who sends him into the fields to feed pigs. We can admire the son's willingness to do odd jobs rather than steal or hit up his father for more cash. But pigs were an abomination to the Jews—these animals were not just physically unclean, but also ceremonially unclean. Nevertheless, the young man is willing to accept a vocation condemned by his religion, just to put food in his stomach.

Hunger forces him to compromise his beliefs and his dignity—in the pigpen he loses his self-respect: "He longed to fill his stomach with the pods that the pigs were eating, but no one gave him anything" (v. 16). The boy discovers that his good-time friends are untrustworthy; now that he is penniless, his buddies are of no help. Destitute, he faces a decision.

WHY STAY IN THE FAR COUNTRY?

Everyone who has blown it comes to a moment of truth—a crisis in which they must make a decision to either turn back or keep going. This young man could have hardened his heart, steeled his mind, and thought, *I'd rather starve than go home and face my father and that goody-two-sandals brother of mine.*

The thought of returning home triggers guilt and shame. How can he look his father in the eye? And how can he return penniless, then suffer the sneers of his older brother, who has a nose-to-the-grindstone reputation and never does anything wrong? No doubt people back home are talking about his father's two sons, the good one who stayed home and worked the farm, and the delinquent who took the old man's money and ran.

He had never cared for the rigors and rules of the farm, and wild living has since inflamed his passions. He isn't even sure he can acclimate himself once again to farm life.

Live or die, there are compelling reasons for him to stay away from his father's house.

WHEN REALITY DAWNS

But this scoundrel has the good sense to do something right after he had done so many things wrong. Rather than making the same old choices and reaping the same old demoralizing consequences, "he came to his senses" (v. 17).

That is a pivotal phrase. We wish we could read that he loved his father so much that he could not bear being separated from him and so chose to return. However, his motives are much less noble. He is hungry. His stomach, not his heart, tells him that going home might be a very good idea. "How many of my father's hired men have food to spare, and here I am starving to death!" (v. 17).

Nevertheless, if the young man did not consider his father to be gracious and forgiving, if he thought that his father was a hard and frugal man who counted offenses and held grudges, then the son would likely have remained in the far country, come what may.

But the father's love cuts both ways: It beckons him to return, but also magnifies his own rebellion. If the young man returns, he will have to face his own guilt and shame in the presence of undeserved love. Grace is often more difficult to accept than the law wielded with a heavy club.

The son prepares a speech: "Father, I have sinned against heaven and against you. I am no longer worthy to be called your son; make me like one of your hired men" (v. 18–19).

You can't help but like this boy. Sure, he blew his money and dignity. Sure, he tarnished the reputation of his father and his family. But the young man makes no rationalizations. He doesn't say, "Well, if were not for my friends—they lied to me and spent my money." Or "It was the recession—unemployment was high, and it cost me everything."

He's blown it and he admits it.

He knows that slavery in his father's house is better than freedom in the far country. And so he sets out, rehearsing his speech with every step.

THE FATHER KEEPS WATCH

Back home, the father has lost all interest in the farm. Often he will put down his tools and stare down the road, hoping for a glimpse of his boy. My wife and I have counseled people whose children have rebelled and live in the far country. The parents tell us that they go to bed at night thinking about their child, and they wake in the morning thinking about their child. Parents can only be as happy as their saddest child.

Although the boy left the father's farm, he never left his father's heart. We read, "But while he was still a long way off, his father saw him and was filled with compassion for him; he ran to his son, threw his arms around him and kissed him" (v. 20). In the original Greek text, "a long way off" is the same word as "the distant country." The father's eyes are searching the whole landscape, longing for a sign of his son's return.

When he spots the young man coming up the road, the father runs to embrace his son. The boy begins his speech, but he is so smothered with kisses that he does not have a chance to finish. He begins, "Father I have sinned…," but his father is not nearly as interested in the confession as he is in having his son back in his arms.

The father shouts, "Quick! Bring the best robe and put it on him. Put a ring on his finger and sandals on his feet.

Bring the fattened calf and kill it. Let's have a feast and celebrate. For this son of mine was dead and is alive again; he was lost and is found" (v. 22–24).

And the party is on.

GOOD NEWS FOR WAYWARD SONS— AND DAUGHTERS

What should we do after we have blown it? Our very first decision should be to hurry back to the arms of our waiting heavenly Father. Every day we delay in the distant country is another day we break His heart. When we are absent, our Father hurts deeply, because He loves deeply. He loves His sons and daughters, and our wisest course is always to take the shortest route home, where we belong.

Those of us who have blown it, and royally so; those who committed sexual sin this week; those of us who have selfishly squandered our lives; those of us who have made promises to change but don't—our first right step is to run back to the Father.

Any reluctance is all on our side. We hesitate because of our shame. We fear our Father's wrath and what He might do if we "turn ourselves in." Or we are angry with the Father and his judgmental children. We tell ourselves that we will return home only when we know we are able to follow the rules of the Father's kingdom. Sometimes we are tempted to return for selfish reasons. Even so, the Father does not chide us but is just glad that we have come back to Him.

THEN THERE'S THE OLDER BROTHER...

The young man of the story learns that it is one thing to reconcile with his father, but quite another to reconcile with the father's children. When the elder brother returns home after a hard day's work and hears a celebration happening, you might expect him to throw down his hoe, grab a party hat, and shout, "Thank God my brother is back!" Instead, he is so angry he refuses to step inside the house. Although he was busy doing his father's work, he was unconcerned about the salvation of others—even the salvation of his own brother.

When we return to the Father, we may have to put up with the "bean counters" who believe that our relationship with God is based on merit.

"How can God use him when he's spent time in jail!"

"God can't bless her because she's divorced!"

"I don't think he's really sincere. How can he be saved?"

When our children were born, my wife and I did not say, "We'll love these children only when they grow up and get a good education and a vocation—something that will make us look good." No, we loved them simply because they were our children. Just so, God loves us quite apart from our performance. Grace is all one-sided: When we come to God, we bring only our great need; He supplies the rest.

So after the younger son had disrespectfully demanded his inheritance and then squandered it in a distant land, why did the father seem so taken with the young man? I believe it is, in part, because the father had finally found someone willing to wear the special robe and the ring that had lain in his treasure chest. He had found a candidate for the sandals that had been waiting on a shelf on the front porch.

The elder brother had, in essence, refused these blessings because he didn't see himself as a son, but as a slave. Work on the farm was all drudgery and no delight. He had become so accustomed to working for the father that he had lost the wonder of his father's love and the joy of service. He saw his father as stingy rather than generous, and he refused to enjoy the blessings that his father had set aside for him.

The older brother served his father for what he could get out of him—a living, food, and a home—not out of love. Frankly, the older son stayed home because he didn't have the nerve to leave. When he criticizes his younger brother for squandering his money on prostitutes (see v. 30), we get a hint of what the older son might have done with *his* share of the inheritance if fear hadn't kept him at home!

Grace is difficult to receive. Those of us who know we have sinned recognize the stench of pigs on our clothes. We hate not only what we have done, but who we are. We think our sin is too great to be welcomed back.

Then there are the "elder brothers" who think they do not need grace. They compare themselves with others and see that they are doing fine, thank you very much. They reject the gracious embrace of the father, instead enduring the farm one day at a time. As long as they look good to others, they think everything is peachy.

But the father speaks to the elder son tenderly. "My child," he says, using the Greek word *teknon*, a tender word for *child,* "you are constantly with me." God loves his children, even when they will not accept their forgiven brothers and sisters. He loves those who are difficult to love, including the self-righteous and judgmental folks who resent the blessings given to prodigals. To the elder brothers the Father says, "Join the party! We will work tomorrow, but tonight we shall celebrate!"

Many prodigals cannot bring themselves to return to

the Father because they cannot face the elder brothers who are quick to judge, quick to criticize, quick to shoot those who are wounded. But we cannot let the attitude of others keep us from the Father's tender embrace. To all those who have blown it, I say, "Hurry to the Father, and don't let the criticism of your elder brothers stop you!"

God waits eagerly for all those who are in the distant country. He will not hesitate to send a famine to get our attention. Addictions, broken relationships, financial reversals, a troubled conscience—all of these are alarm bells to remind us that the Father is waiting. Our mess is often God's message, His megaphone inviting us to return home, where we belong.

Yes, those who return will need to adjust and adhere to the Father's ways, but tonight He is saying, "Come home to Me! Let us feast and enjoy the banquet I have prepared for you. We will talk tomorrow about tomorrow."

To the person whose clothes bear the stench of sin, the Father declares, "I have a clean robe waiting for you." For the disgruntled person who does not understand grace, He says, "Come join the party."

To all of us He says, "My arms are open."

No matter how bad you have blown it, the Father is waiting.

Chapter Two

THE GUILT
YOU CAN'T
WISH AWAY

"Tell me man-to-man: Is there a way out or isn't there? If there is, I want to know about it; if there isn't, I'm going to blow my brains out."

The man who spoke was a bisexual who had just learned that he had passed on the AIDS virus to his wife. She was not about to forgive his secret liaisons, his deceptions and lies. And now she was infected with a fatal disease.

Ryan (not his real name) told me that he attended church regularly and made a habit of confessing his sins, but that he had no real assurance of forgiveness. Desperate though he was, Ryan did not know how to "connect" with God. The thought of death frightened him, for he was convinced that if there was an afterlife, hell surely awaited him. Yet in his misery, suicide had become an increasingly attractive option.

As best I could, I explained to Ryan that he had three distinct but related problems that needed to be resolved. First, he needed to face the fact that he was separated from God, as all of us are by virtue of being human. Objectively, we have all sinned and are guilty before God, and until that barrier of sin is removed, we cannot know God or delight in fellowship with Him.

Second, there was the matter of guilt and regret—the despair and depression that overwhelmed Ryan as his conscience screamed at him that he had messed up, big-time. These feelings were accompanied by raging self-condemnation and a wish to die. But Ryan's conscience could only be cleared after his relationship with God had been rectified. Step one had to come before step two.

Finally, there was the anger of his wife whom he had betrayed. This would take time to repair. And quite frankly, he might never be reconciled to his wife. But yes, with God, life was still worth living.

Why didn't Ryan's confession of sin give him peace? I explained to him that we do not become Christians just by confessing our sins. Many people who confess their sins to God or a priest are not "born again," as Jesus said we must be to enter the kingdom of heaven (John 3:3). For one thing, it is not possible for us to remember *all* of our sins; we usually remember only the ones that continue to trouble us. And we might well have committed many sins of which we are unaware. Remember, God's standards are much higher than ours. Yes, as Christians, we do confess our sins, but that's not how we become members of God's family.

What this man needed was one act of God by which he would become one of God's sons. He needed to have *all* of his sins—whether he remembered them or not—taken away, so that he could "connect" with his Creator. Ryan needed a personal sin-bearer, One who had lived without sin but who paid the price for everything Ryan had ever done. Ryan needed to know that he could be welcomed by God on the merit of Jesus' sacrifice alone. Thankfully, God had made provision and could do for this man what he desperately needed done.

When you prepare to board a plane, the airline's agents do not ask whether you have had a good day or a bad day. They do not ask whether you feel depressed or happy. What they want to know is whether you have a ticket. Just so, when we accept Christ as our Savior through faith, He is our ticket to God.

The issue is not whether we feel worthy of this gift. We aren't. The issue is not whether we feel guilty. We are. The issue is not the number or relative size of our sins. Even so-called good people are separated from God both by nature and by choice. Those who have fallen the farthest at least have this advantage: They *know* they are desperately in need of God's forgiveness, unlike those who see themselves as pretty decent people. God loves to help those who know how bad off they really are.

Ryan—bless him—had this advantage. His guilt and despair were driving him to God. The condemning inner voice motivated him to ask how he could find peace with God and with himself. But it is not just the sexually immoral person who feels the deadening grip of guilt. So does the alcoholic; so does the gambler; so does the woman who has had an abortion. So does anyone who struggles with a recurring sin. So do all of us who have not lived up to what we know is right.

Ryan accepted Christ as his Savior. When he knew that he had been forgiven by God, a tremendous weight was lifted from his shoulders. But that was not the end of his struggle with guilt and self-condemnation. Even after God had taken his sin away, his conscience still plagued him.

As sinners, we all have a God-sized problem.

Thankfully, there is a God-sized solution.

CLEARED OF WRONGDOING

The Old Testament prophet Zechariah had a vision that illustrates both our dilemma and God's answer to our guilt. In Zechariah's vision, a priest stood before God with shame, but walked away declared as righteous as God Himself!

His story can be ours.

> Then he showed me Joshua the high priest standing before the angel of the LORD, and Satan standing at his right side to accuse him. Now Joshua was dressed in filthy clothes as he stood before the angel.
>
> ZECHARIAH 3:1, 3

Visualize the scene. See how the priest is dressed. His filthy clothes mirror the content of his heart—they reflect his guilt before God. Joshua is unclean. He is dirty, guilty, and quite unable to do anything about it.

If his heart were being compared to that of a common criminal, Joshua would look much better. Even if he were standing alongside members of our own congregation, he would prove more righteous than the rest. But Joshua is in the presence of someone far more righteous than he. He is in the presence of the "angel of the LORD."

Let's take a closer look at this "angel." We have a clue as to who He is when we hear Him say, "The LORD rebuke you, Satan! The LORD, who has chosen Jerusalem, rebuke you!" (v. 2). And as we shall see, this "angel of the Lord" has the ability to forgive sins. Biblical scholars generally agree that *"the* angel of the Lord" (as opposed to *an* angel of the Lord) refers to Christ before Bethlehem.

Joshua is standing in the presence of Jesus.

The fact is, if God were not so holy, our guilt might be manageable. But the divine standard is the Divine One Himself!

What do you suppose Joshua wants to do in this moment? Given his druthers, I'm sure he would run from the presence of the Lord. But he just stands there, burning with shame. *And he is just as guilty as he feels!* Likewise, we stand condemned in the presence of holiness, the presence of the One whose purity we must match. We stand exposed, spiritually naked.

But the same Jesus who judges Joshua also covers him:

> The angel said to those who were standing before him, "Take off his filthy clothes." Then he said to Joshua, "See, I have taken away your sin, and I will put rich garments on you."
>
> ZECHARIAH 3:4

So Joshua's filthy garments are discarded, but he is not left naked. Clean clothes, "rich garments," are put on his shoulders. He can now stand before the Lord without shame.

Ponder this: The issue is not the greatness or the multitude of our sin but rather the beauty of the robes that cover us. We might well ask, *Just how filthy are Joshua's garments? Of what sins is he guilty?* Interesting questions, but they're irrelevant because his "filth" is fully covered.

Reformation pastor George Spalatin was immersed in grief and guilt—he could not be consoled after giving a parishioner bad moral advice. Upon hearing of Spalatin's condition, Martin Luther took up his pen and wrote to his friend. In his letter, Luther did not minimize Spalatin's sin, but rather magnified God's grace. Jesus, he said, did not die only for our "childish sins" but for our "real, great, grievous and damnable transgressions and iniquities, yea…the very greatest and most shocking sins." As Luther wrote to his friend, Christ is a real Savior for real sinners.[2]

And so standing in the presence of Jesus, Joshua is acquitted.

But the presence of Satan gives this story a twist. He has no stomach for reconciliation but is there to sow division. Heaven calls him "the accuser of our brothers, who accuses them before our God day and night" (Revelation 12:10). Satan is trying to separate Joshua from his God by leveling charges against the priest before the Lord.

Before we even consider the grounds for these accusations, let's think this through. Who is making these accusations? Isn't it the one who is the very *embodiment* of sin? If Joshua is dirty, Satan is dirtier still. If Joshua is unclean, Satan is doubly so. No wonder demons, who have the nature of their leader, are frequently called "unclean spirits." They are totally filthy without a hint of goodness or a whiff of kindness.

But Satan is not only the embodiment of sin, he is also the *instigator* of sin. He tempted Adam and Eve to sin and continues to lead humanity astray. Satan and his minions lure us into sin so that he can turn around and accuse us of being sinners! He is like a man who is both a firefighter and an arsonist—he constantly appears at disasters that he has helped create.

So what is Satan's motivation? Hatred. Hatred of God and hatred of God's people. Blinded by rage, consumed with jealousy, and facing a humiliating future, he reminds us of our guilt and shame as we stand in the presence of God. "Just look at your dirty clothes," he says. "You say God has forgiven you. Really? Just remember what you did. You don't *feel* forgiven, do you? God is so furious with you, you ought to just go away."

Satan wants to convince us of our hopelessness. He wants us to turn away from God and commit additional sins to deaden the pain created by our earlier sins. The evil one wants to separate us from fellowship with God, cutting us off from the blessing of a clear conscience. He wants to skew our perspective, to make our sin look bigger than God's grace.

Thankfully, the Lord takes up our cause. He rebukes the devil's accusations. To be sure, we *are* great sinners, but God makes a huge distinction between what we deserve and the grace He will give us. Because of Jesus, God removes our sin and declares us to be as righteous as Himself, and He dresses us in His clothes.

CONVICTION VS. GUILT

The clean garments Joshua receives from the Lord represent the gift of righteousness we receive when we accept Jesus Christ as our sin-bearer. We are acquitted by God and declared to be His children (see Romans 8:16–17).

But that does not mean our battle with sin is over. Guilt plagues the non-Christian, but often it dogs us as Christians, too. The difference is this: Having received Christ as our sin-bearer, we now have a means by which our conscience can be cleansed. We confess our sins, not in order to become God's children—for now we are His children forever—but because we want our fellowship with the Father to be fully restored. When my children were young and they disobeyed me, they came to ask my forgiveness.

Not so they could be reinstated as my children, but to restore our broken fellowship.

We must distinguish between the accusations of Satan and the conviction given to us by the Holy Spirit. If you confuse the two, you will continually focus on your sinfulness and your joy will always be on hold. What if Joshua had believed Satan's accusations? What if he had listened only to the voice that told him he was filthy, the voice that condemns and damns us all? Joshua would have sunk into self-hatred, despair, and hopelessness.

When we belong to God's family, the Holy Spirit convicts us of sin for which we must ask forgiveness; but once we have confessed the sin, the matter is settled. We are forgiven. And yet Satan continues to accuse us of sin that has been forgiven, agitating us about matters that God says have been taken care of.

However, we can counter his accusations with this:

Who will bring any charge against those whom God has chosen? It is God who justifies. Who is he that condemns? Christ Jesus, who died—more than that, who was raised to life—is at the right hand of God and is also interceding for us.

ROMANS 8:33–34

So we can say with all confidence, "The Lord rebuke you, Satan!"

The story of Joshua the priest tells us that our guilt should drive us *toward* God, not away from Him. When we have done something wrong, we must suppress our natural instinct to run and hide and instead come into God's presence as we are, without excuses or pretense.

My point is this: *The guilt you feel is not God trying to push you away from Him. Guilt is God trying to put His arms around you.*

WILL YOU REJECT HIS GIFT?

Perhaps what amazes me most about this passage is that God not only chooses to forgive us who have sinned against Him, He chooses to *honor* us. Joshua is not merely given new garments, but a princely turban is brought out and placed upon his head. He is restored to ministry and given charge over the Lord's house and courts.

I've recently heard testimony from a former heroin addict who had served time for armed robbery. After he accepted God's forgiveness for his many sins, the man was hired as a supervisor in a Christian organization. He said, "The fact that I, a scumbag, was told that I could be used of God, drove me to my knees in thankfulness."

But what if we refuse or are reluctant to accept God's gift of grace? What if the prodigal son had lingered a while longer in the distant country? What if Joshua had said, "No thanks, Lord, I am a sinner and don't deserve new clothes, so I'll just wear what I have on"?

The Shawshank Redemption is a movie about prison life in Maine in the 1940s and the following decades. The story centers on the journey of two men's hearts through the trials and temptations of surviving year after year in the penitentiary. When they receive news of a friend committing suicide *after he is released from prison,* Red, perhaps the wisest and most seasoned of the inmates, explains what happens when you live within the prison walls too long: "These walls are kind of funny. First you hate 'em, then you get used to 'em. Enough time passes, gets so you depend on them."

The same thing happens when you're a slave to sin. You begin by hating your dirty clothes—and the anger, addictions, and deception that go with them—but after a while, you get used to them. And then you begin to find comfort in them. Eventually, you *need* them. That is the most tragic day of all—the day you prefer slavery to freedom. The day you prefer your permanently stained clothes to the clean royal robes God has waiting for you.

Do not delay a moment longer. Do not grow accustomed to your sin. The Father is waiting, and He has rich garments ready for all who will come to Him through Christ. Be assured that no stain is permanent and no person is beyond hope in the presence of the Lord.

If you have never transferred your trust to Christ alone, I encourage you to pray this prayer right now that expresses your heart's desire:

Father, I thank You for sending Jesus Christ
to be my substitute.
I receive Him as my personal Savior,
trusting Him to take my sin away.
Thank You for the assurance that when
I transfer my trust to Jesus,
You will receive me as one of Your own.
His merit becomes my merit when I depend
on Him as my sin-bearer.
I pray this in Jesus' name. Amen.

"Yet to all who received him, to those who believed in his name, he gave the right to become children of God."

JOHN 1:12

Chapter Three

WHAT GOD DOES WITH FORGIVEN SIN

A woman who had had an abortion said that, for the past four years, every time she saw a child who was the age her child would have been, she became gripped with guilt and regret. She would again relive what she had done in killing her unborn infant. As a Christian, she had confessed her sin many times, but the guilt would often return with a vengeance.

Sin is deceitful. It does not announce beforehand how

much guilt will accompany a particular act of disobedience. This woman had no idea that four years later she would still be haunted by her wanton desire to be free from the responsibilities of motherhood.

Suppose you were to steal a million dollars and get away with it. Most likely your conscience would not allow you to enjoy the spoils. Sociopaths enjoy their crimes only because their consciences have become deadened to any stimulus. The rest of us can only try to stifle the voice that insists on reminding us of our past transgressions.

Such memories cannot be cordoned off; you can't keep them on one side of your soul while the other part remains at peace. You try to concentrate, but your mind flits back to your troubled conscience. David said, "My sin is always before me" (Psalm 51:3). Our sins—particularly certain kinds of sins—are often on our minds when we're at the office, when we drive home, and even when we are trying to worship in church.

We don't have the ability to wipe the human heart clean. We cannot enter the crevices of our psyche and clear up the mess. Talk shows and "reality" television programs claim that airing our dirty laundry before millions of people is a cleansing catharsis, but it is like washing linen in mud. The polluted human heart cannot wash itself clean.

What We Do with Our Guilt

We cannot unlearn guilt, nor can it be washed away with alcohol or drugs. Try as we might, we cannot totally silence the voice of conscience because intuitively we believe that we are being condemned by a higher law. A law beyond our control. A law to which we must answer.

Often, we try to manage our guilt by comparing ourselves to someone who is "worse" than we are, those who are guilty of greater sins—the guy in the next office who cheats on his wife, the abusive husband down the street, or the woman in Accounting who recently ran off with some serious money. Sure, we've done some bad things, *but just look at them.*

Sometimes we try to silence the conscience by compensating for our sins with good deeds. I have a friend who told me that, growing up, whenever he mowed the lawn without being told, his mother would say, "Well, what have you been up to *now*?" And there *are* those who perform social work, hoping by their good deeds to "even the score" and prove to themselves that they're not as bad as their vices imply.

Others bargain with God by trying to punish themselves for their misdeeds. A man who fathered a child he had never seen told me, "For twenty-seven years I believed that I could not be forgiven unless I was punished." In the

Philippines, members of a cult known as the Flagelantes subject themselves to the same kind of torture Christ endured. Some actually have themselves nailed to crosses.

Still the voice of conscience cries out, *There is more to pay!*

Some who are plagued by guilt develop a propensity for "accidents" or a harmful habit, harboring a secret wish to die young. William Justice tells of a brilliant young man who talked about his use of heroin. When Justice asked why he did it, the boy replied, "You ought to know the answer to that question without me telling you.... I feel so bad about some of the things I've done, I want to die. I don't have the guts to pick up a gun and blow my brains out, so I just do it the slow way with drugs. I feel that I've gotta pay for all I've done wrong."[3]

Justice writes:

For every failure to live up to some ought, there is the tendency to punish one's self in such a manner as to produce another failure! And every failure produces the response, *I ought not to have failed!* Having failed, I punish myself in such a manner as to produce a further sense of failure.[4]

Like a snowball rolling down a hill, this "cycle of the damned" picks up momentum, increasing in intensity. Our inner judge keeps crying, *More! More!* but no matter how much we pay, we can never pay enough and any relief is temporary at best, fatal at worst.

WHAT GOD DOES WITH OUR SIN

Why do we find it so difficult to accept God's forgiveness? First of all, we must still live with the inevitable consequences of sin, the domino effects that our actions have set into motion. The man who repents of his adultery still must reconcile with his wife or face divorce. The forgiven alcoholic who has lost his job must still face life without a paycheck. Forgiveness will not bring back the aborted child. Forgiven people sometimes have been sentenced to die in a gas chamber.

Another reason so many of us are reluctant to accept forgiveness is because we think we deserve to feel guilty. We think, *It's not fair for me to be free of guilt, given the wretch I am.* But guilt can never pay for our sins. Guilt of the most torturous kind does not commend us to God—we don't make ourselves any more presentable to God by enduring the misery we know we deserve. Our guilt cannot add to the value of Christ's death on the cross for us.

In light of God's grace, it is sheer arrogance for us to hang on to our guilt. C. S. Lewis put it like this: "I think that if God forgives us we must forgive ourselves.

Otherwise it is almost like setting up ourselves as a higher tribunal than Him."[5]

We might be troubled by our forgiven sin, but God is not. Because of the death and resurrection of Jesus, our confessed sin has been so thoroughly put away that it no longer presents a barrier to our fellowship with the Almighty. Forgiven sin is only what we make it to be: Either we can allow it to plague our conscience, or we can send it to where God has already put it.

When I was a boy of about ten, my sister gave me a Magic Slate. I would draw pictures and write words and phrases on it, then lift the transparent page and watch what I had written disappear without a trace. Just so, our lives are written on God's tablet, but He can blot out the words we have said, the thoughts we have entertained, and the deeds we have done. Yes, the consequences of our actions may remain, but our sins themselves are no longer visible. God has put them out of His sight.

The Bible describes in several different ways how wondrously and completely God dealt with our sin.

He Covers Our Sin

"Blessed is he whose transgressions are forgiven, whose sins are covered" (Psalm 32:1). Imagine two roads: One is clean and well traveled; the other is wretched, with deep ruts that veer off into a ditch. When a heavy snowfall blankets the two roads, both are equally covered. Just so, our sins, big and small, are equally covered by God: "Though your sins are like scarlet, they shall be as white as snow; though they are red as crimson, they shall be like wool" (Isaiah 1:18).

David prayed that he would be washed, "whiter than the snow." I've often wondered how anything could be whiter than blinding, glistening snow. Then I learned that snowflakes are created when particles of dust, called *nuclei*, attract moisture and crystallize. The snow that appears to us as wholly pure actually has bits of contamination visible through a microscope. When God forgives us, every trace of impurity is removed; there is no contamination in the beautiful righteousness credited to our account!

Charles Spurgeon illustrated in a moving sermon the lengths God will go to in covering our sins:

> Man piles a mountain of sin, but God will match it, and He upheaves a loftier mountain of grace; man heaps up a still [larger] hill of sin, but the Lord overtops it with ten times more grace; and so the contest continues till at last the mighty God plucks up the mountains by the roots and buries man's sin beneath them as a fly might be buried beneath an Alp. Abundant sin is no barrier to the superabundant grace of God.[6]

He Removes Our Sin

"As far as the east is from the west, so far has he removed our transgressions from us" (Psalm 103:12). A man who had committed adultery told me that although his wife forgave him, "when we had an argument she would always rub my nose in the dirt." God doesn't rub our noses in the dirt. In fact, the dirt has been removed from His sight. Your sins might still be on your mind, but they are not on His! He says, "I have swept away your offenses like a cloud, your sins like the morning mist" (Isaiah 44:22).

A man was walking on a long stretch of sand beside the seashore, and when he looked back, he marveled at how his path strayed this way and that. *Just like my life,* he thought, *every step is crooked.* But hours later when the man walked back to his lodging, he could find no trace of the footprints he had left. The tide had come in and washed away the indentations in the sand. The clean moist surface before him was a reminder that the man did not have to let his past control his future. He had been given a second chance.

The prophet Micah wrote this about God's astounding grace: "You will again have compassion on us; you will tread our sins underfoot and hurl all our iniquities into the depths of the sea" (Micah 7:19). In other words, God throws our sins into the deep blue sea and then puts up a sign: NO FISHING.

He Cleanses Our Conscience

David, plagued by a troubled conscience prayed, "Wash away all my iniquity and cleanse me from my sin.... Cleanse me with hyssop, and I will be clean; wash me, and I will be whiter than snow" (Psalm 51:2, 7).

Here is a promise that we all should know by memory: "If we confess our sins, He is faithful and just to forgive us our sins and to cleanse us from all unrighteousness" (1 John 1:9, NKJV). Notice here that two blessings are ours when we confess our sins: (1) We are forgiven—objectively, our sin is taken away—and (2) subjectively, we are cleansed—that is, our defiled conscience is made clean.

"What will I do with my guilty heart?" a woman asked me. "I can't take steel wool to my heart and scrub it." How right she was. Even the most extra-strength detergent cannot get down to the nitty-gritty level of the conscience. There is no cure for deep regret, for alienation from God, or for self-loathing. Only God is able to reach down to the depth of our psyche and scrub it clean.

A woman who had been immoral in her youth still suffered from guilt and regret over her past sins. "I'm sure you confessed your sins" I said.

"Oh yes, I have confessed those sins a thousand times," she replied.

I pointed out that we cannot clear our consciences by

confessing the same sins again and again. Indeed the very act of "reconfession" is proof that we lack faith that God is "faithful and just to forgive."

When nagging pangs of guilt return, we must affirm that our sins are already forgiven. Guilt serves a purpose in that it leads us to confess our sins to God; but once we have accepted His forgiveness, guilt serves no useful purpose. God says you're forgiven. Nevertheless, Satan likes to keep pricking our conscience.

So whose word are you going to believe?

We *must* side with God in this struggle.

During the temptation in the wilderness, Jesus used Scripture to silence the enemy. When Satan whispers his accusations in our ear, we need to answer him—and our conscience—with God's Word. I suggest you memorize Psalm 32 and quote it often.

He Forgets Our Sin

God said of Himself, "I, even I, am he who blots out your transgressions, for my own sake, and remembers your sins no more" (Isaiah 43:25). This is not to say that God is living in denial as we humans have a tendency to do. To say that God does not remember our sins means that He no longer takes them into account. They are no longer an issue between us. The prophet Isaiah wrote, "In your love you kept me from the pit of destruction; you have put all my sins behind your back" (Isaiah 38:17).

I've written books in longhand, but I like my computer and word processing software, particularly because of such technological advantages as the "delete" key. (I used it twice while writing the previous paragraph.) What an embarrassment it would be if everything that I have ever written were printed as I originally wrote it! I am constantly misspelling words, composing poorly formed sentences, and spouting ideas that need refinement. My "delete" key is a lifesaver!

I'm thankful that when God puts our sin away, He hits the "delete" key.

COMPREHENSIVE COVERAGE

Either we can allow God to cover our sin, or we will likely do all we can to *cover it up*. Mention the biblical figure of David, and most people will remember him as the young man who slew Goliath and later, when he was king, committed adultery. When David learned that Bathsheba was pregnant with his child, did he confess his sin? No, first he tried to deceive her husband, Uriah the Hittite, into believing that the child was his own. When that plan fell through, David had Uriah killed. No one has ever gone to greater lengths to cover his sin, and yet no man's sin has ever received greater exposure!

Our lies, our self-justification, our favorable comparisons to others—it is impossible to exaggerate the amount of mental energy devoted to managing guilt through denials, inappropriate silence, and pretense. But God will never be a party to our cover-ups: "He who conceals his sins does not prosper, but whoever confesses and renounces them finds mercy" (Proverbs 28:13).

The longer we are dishonest with God, with others, and with ourselves, the longer we postpone the blessing of God. In his classic allegory *The Pilgrim's Progress*, John Bunyan likens sin to a burden on the conscience that can only be removed by God. We aren't doing God any favors when we try to manage our sin on our own. Instead, we honor Him when we admit that we need not only His help, but His intervention. A clear conscience is a gift that only He can give.

In the end, forgiven sin has only as much power as we let it have. Or as much power as we let Satan have with it. Yes, the memories of our sin might come to mind. We may experience some of the old guilt and self-condemnation. But we must respond by affirming, *God has spoken on the matter, and I believe His Word.*

The woman who has had an abortion and has been forgiven must affirm that her sin has been covered, removed, and forgotten by our loving God. So must the converted alcoholic and the repentant criminal.

A couple of years ago, a student of mine gave me this powerful story by Joshua Harris:

> In that place between wakefulness and dreams, I found myself in the room. There were no distinguishing features save for the one wall covered with small index-card files.
>
> They were like the ones in libraries that list titles by author or subject in alphabetical order. But these files, which stretched from floor to ceiling and seemingly endlessly in either direction, had very different headings....
>
> I knew exactly where I was. This lifeless room with its small files was a crude catalog system for my life. Here were written the actions of my every moment, big and small, in a detail my memory couldn't match.
>
> A sense of wonder and curiosity, coupled with horror, stirred within me as I began randomly opening files and exploring their contents. Some brought joy and sweet memories; others a sense of shame and regret so intense that I would look over my shoulder to see if anyone was watching....

The titles ranged from the mundane to the outright weird: "Books I Have Read," "Lies I Have Told," "Comfort I Have Given," "Jokes I Have Laughed At." Some were almost hilarious in their exactness: "Things I've Yelled at My Brothers." Others I couldn't laugh at: "Things I Have Done in Anger," "Things I Have Muttered Under My Breath at My Parents." Each was written in my own handwriting. Each signed with my signature.

When I pulled out the file marked "Songs I Have Listened To," I shut it, shamed, not so much by the quality of music, but more by the vast amount of time I knew that file represented.

When I came to a file marked "Lustful Thoughts," I felt a chill run through my body. I pulled the file out only an inch, not willing to test its size, and drew out a card.... I felt sick to think that such a moment had been recorded.

Suddenly I felt an almost animal rage. One thought dominated my mind: *No one must ever see these cards! I have to destroy them!* In an insane frenzy I yanked the file out. I had to empty it and burn the cards. But as I took the file at one end and began pounding it on the floor, I could not dislodge a single card. I became desperate and pulled out a card, only to find it as strong as steel when I tried to tear it.

Defeated and utterly helpless, I let out a long, self-pitying sigh. And then I saw it. The title bore "People I Have Shared the Gospel With." The handle was brighter than those around it, newer, almost unused. I pulled on its handle and a small box not more than three inches long fell into my hands. I could count the cards it contained on one hand.

I began to weep. Sobs so deep that the hurt started in my stomach and shook through me. I fell on my knees and cried. I cried out of shame, from the overwhelming shame of it all. The rows of file shelves swirled in my tear-filled eyes. No one must ever, ever know of this room. I must lock it up and hide the key.

But then as I pushed away the tears, I saw Him. *No, please, not Him. Not here. Oh, anyone but Jesus.*

I watched helplessly as He began to open the files and read the cards. I couldn't bear to watch His response. And in the moments I could bring myself to look at His face, I saw a sorrow deeper than my own....

Finally He turned and looked at me from

across the room. He looked at me with pity in His eyes. I dropped my head, covered my face with my hands, and began to cry again. He walked over and put His arm around me. He could have said so many things. But He didn't say a word. He just cried with me.

Then He got up and walked back to the wall of files. Starting at one end of the room, He took out a file and, one by one, began to sign His name over mine on each card.

"No!" I shouted, rushing to Him. All I could find to say was "No, no," as I pulled the card from Him. His name shouldn't be on these cards. But there it was, written in red so rich, so dark, so alive. The name of Jesus covered mine. It was written with His blood.

He gently took the card back. He smiled a sad smile and continued to sign the cards. I don't think I'll ever understand how He did it so quickly, but the next instant it seemed I heard Him close the last file and walk back to my side. He placed His hand on my shoulder and said, "It is finished."

I stood up, and He led me out of the room. There was no lock on its door. There were still cards to be written.[7]

God is not mad at us; we are mad at ourselves. To the person who says, "I can accept God's forgiveness, but I can't forgive myself," I say this: If the God of the universe says you are forgiven, *who are you* to withhold forgiveness from yourself? God knows your situation. He knows what you've done and the consequences of your actions. And He is equal to the task of ridding you of the self-hatred that may be destroying you.

Let me suggest that you pray right now, insisting that you take God at His word. "But where sin increased, grace increased all the more" (Romans 5:20).

Chapter Four

So You've Done
It Again!

"I can't come to God with *that* sin one more time. Why should I think He would forgive me *again*?"

These were the words of a young Christian man who had vowed to God that if he were forgiven for his one-night stand with a girl he scarcely knew, he would never do such a thing again. He had begged God's forgiveness, and although he struggled with his memories, his conscience had ceased the worst of its torments. But now, less than a week later, he found himself in the same predicament. He had broken his promise to "never do it again," adding to his guilt and remorse. The young man also was beginning to realize that he could not trust himself—for all he knew, he'd do it again.

So how many times can we count on God to forgive us?

We've learned that when we embrace Christ as our Savior, our sin—all of it—is taken away by God. Yet, as believers, we must confess the sins that come to our attention if we are to enjoy fellowship with the Almighty. Confession is a discipline our heavenly Father requires in order for us to have a clear conscience and to live in obedience to His expectations.

Repeating the same sinful behavior is most discouraging. Who of us has not told God that if He would forgive us *just one more time,* we would never do it again…only to blow it once more? A man who seemingly could not quit gambling away his paycheck told me, "My Christian life is on hold. Someday I hope to get back in fellowship with God when I know I can hold out and not return to my addictive lifestyle."

The purpose of this chapter is not to discuss how we can stop repeating the same destructive behaviors; that would be the subject of another book. My aim is more modest. I hope merely to answer the question of whether we should keep asking God to forgive us during those times when we are spinning our wheels, blowing it time after time.

LIKE LAMBS TO THE PASTURE

As Christians, we've all experienced struggles with repeated sin. The New Testament describes this battle in vivid language:

> For the sinful nature desires what is contrary to the Spirit, and the Spirit what is contrary to the sinful nature. They are in conflict with each other, so that you do not do what you want.
>
> GALATIANS 5:17

Even as believers, our soul is a stage where spirit and flesh, light and darkness, and good and evil vie for control. The good news is that when we accept Christ as our Savior, our deepest desires are transformed, so that we love what we once cared little about.

Consider this biblical illustration: The sheep is a clean animal that avoids garbage and is constantly trying to keep itself clean. In fact, the sheep prefers still water to flowing water, so that it can drink without getting its hair wet. The pig, on the other hand, is an unclean animal that likes garbage and mud. You can wash a pig, dress it in a tux, and take it to a clean stall, but the pig will find a way to get dirty the moment you turn your back. However, if you could take the nature of a lamb and implant it into the pig, the swine would be changed from the inside out. Soon the pig would go out of its way to avoid mud puddles and gravitate toward the greenest part of the pasture.

Just so, when we are "born again," God changes us on the inside, and our desires and motivations change. We begin to love Someone whom we have not seen. And the greater our love for our Lord, the more deeply we are grieved when we dismay Him by sinning. Indeed, our greatest motivation toward holy living is that we do not wish to displease the One we love.

Yet, as Christians, we can and do sin, sometimes seriously so. But the "misery factor" in the aftermath of our sin is greatly increased. To live in conscious violation of our Father's will makes us unhappy souls. We intensely dislike our behavior, and our repeated sin becomes a huge burden to us. So when we commit the same sins as those committed by non-Christians, we are acting contrary to who we are. We know that we are living more like sons of the flesh when, in point of fact, we are sons of God.

But—and this is important—*no matter how often we blow it, we must return to the Father.* We must never let our failures keep us from God's forgiving grace.

READY TO CONFESS

After we've blown it, we face a choice: Do we turn inward, hoping to cope with failure on our own and accepting whatever consequences come our way? Or do we return to the Father to be forgiven one more time? Do we return, even if we suspect that this will not be the last time we're going to have to ask forgiveness for this particular stupid behavior?

Christians really have no options on this one. We must return to the Father as quickly as we can, in humble confession. We cannot let our sins keep us from God, but rather we must use them to drive us to Him. You can judge how far you have come in your spiritual life by how much time elapses between when you blow it and when you return to God in confession.

We say, "Lord, how can I face You again with the same sin?" But He replies, "What sin? I put your sin out of My sight. I must say, your memory is better than Mine!"

We should never let sins fester within our conscience. We must hurry to the Father, sorry that we have disobeyed Him but knowing that we will displease Him even more if we will not humbly come to Him to ask for forgiveness. Better to return to the Father a thousand times than to stay away waiting for a more convenient time to repent.

The more deliberate the sin, the more we know we

have treated our Father with contempt. But we cannot allow our regrets to keep us from asking that our fellowship with Him be restored. Conscious sin demands immediate, heartfelt confession.

Let's return to this promise once again: "If we confess our sins, He is faithful and just to forgive us our sins and to cleanse us from all unrighteousness" (1 John 1:9, NKJV).

What does it mean to "confess our sins"?

Confession means that we *agree* with God. We agree that we have sinned. We agree that we are responsible for our sins. And we agree that God has the right to rid us of this sin. Confession means that I come to God without self-justification, without blaming others, and without excuses (no matter how carefully crafted).

A woman in South America brought her dirty laundry to the river, where the women of the village washed their families' clothes. The woman was so ashamed of her dirty clothes in the presence of others that she left them in her basket, then dipped the basket in the water several times before returning home. Sometimes that is the way we confess our sins. We prefer to make a general admission of guilt without listing the details of our offenses. But God demands complete honesty. That takes some time and a large dose of submission, but without it, our conscience will remain uneasy.

The danger is that we will try to find some reason

within ourselves *why* God should forgive us. We're tempted to think, *I really am a good person at heart. What I did was bad, but there are others who are worse than me.* Or we might think, *I had a wonderful time worshipping on Sunday—that proves my failure is not really who I am.*

No, we must come, cap in hand, without comparisons, without rationalizations, and without excuses. We come before Him to receive the grace we in *no way* deserve.

After we have confessed our sins, we should say, "Father, Jesus is my righteousness. Don't look at me, for I am sinful. Just see me as You see Jesus." This is, after all, why God can take us back after we've blown it a thousand times.

> Set your minds on things above, not on earthly things. For you died, and your life is now hidden with Christ in God.
>
> COLOSSIANS 3:2–3

You see, if we have accepted Christ to be our Savior, God chooses to accept us as if we were His own Son. Jesus' good works are counted as our good works; His perfections become our perfections. Confession means that we gratefully admit one more time that, because of Jesus, our fellowship with God that was hopelessly broken has been fully restored.

And what if we have committed sins of which we are not aware? If we confess those that God brings to our attention, we will be forgiven for those we either don't remember or don't recognize: "But if we walk in the light, as he is in the light, we have fellowship with one another, and the blood of Jesus, his Son, purifies us from all sin" (1 John 1:7).

Continuous confession is the path to continuous fellowship, and it is the path to continuous growth in our Christian life and experience. Keeping our accounts current with our Father demonstrates our love and respect for Him. He takes our sin seriously, and so should we.

No matter how grievously we have sinned, we must never hesitate to return to the Father again and again. Each time we will receive forgiveness and grace to help in time of need. There is more grace in God's heart than there is sin in our past. Spurgeon put it this way: "God is more ready to forgive me than I am ready to offend."

A WORD OF WARNING

Since God is so willing to forgive us, isn't it safe to sin?

"If I sin in a big way, I can be forgiven in a big way and tell of God's grace in a big way." Those were the words of a young Christian man, as he tried to justify his sexual relationship with a married woman. He knew he had blown it, but could see no compelling reason to quit.

When we are tempted to sin while counting on the mercy of God, we stand in danger of taking deliberate advantage of the grace of God. Thankfully, God does invite us to bounce back into fellowship with Him, but we have to guard against presumption, the notion that we can take sin lightly because of God's grace.

Paul the apostle knew that teaching grace risked giving the impression that we, as Christians, had a license to sin. He feared that some would say that since forgiveness was free, sin could be enjoyed without undue concern. Like the man who was cheating on his wife said, "Of course, God will forgive me—that's His job!" Yes, some will try to take advantage of God's abundant grace. But the answer is not to minimize grace; rather, we must understand what grace is intended to do in our lives.

Paul writes, "You, my brothers, were called to be free. But do not use your freedom to indulge the sinful nature; rather, serve one another in love" (Galatians 5:13). Grace should create within us a passion for Christ that is greater than our passion to sin. When properly understood, grace motivates us to holiness, not to carelessness, in our walk with God. Like any good father, God disciplines us when we go astray. He not only lets us experience the consequences of our sin, but the Holy Spirit keeps reminding us that we must turn from our wanderings and come to our Father who waits for our obedience.

Indeed, there are serious consequences if we should take His grace for granted:

Do not be deceived: God cannot be mocked. A man reaps what he sows. The one who sows to please his sinful nature, from that nature will reap destruction; the one who sows to please the Spirit, from the Spirit will reap eternal life. Let us not become weary in doing good, for at the proper time we will reap a harvest if we do not give up.

GALATIANS 6:7–9

God has invested our works with certain consequences. If we choose to serve ourselves, we will experience one set of results; if we choose to serve God, we will have another set of results.

As any amateur gardener knows, the soil will yield what you plant there. We sow to the flesh when we watch sensual television shows that stir lustful passions; we sow to the flesh when we resort to anger to resolve conflict; we sow to the flesh when we let the love of money dictate our values and lifestyle. Remember, confession and forgiveness do not necessarily stop the harvest—certain seeds sown will bear bitter fruit, even if we have confessed our sin.

Unfortunately, when we are tempted to sin, most of the consequences remain hidden. We plant in one season and harvest in another. Some things are certain: First, sin earns wages; second, it pays wages; and third, it *insists* on paying (see Romans 6:23). And as life draws to a close for us, we will certainly reap a harvest of some kind, for a harvest is inevitable:

> "As the weeds are pulled up and burned in the fire, so it will be at the end of the age. The Son of Man will send out his angels, and they will weed out of his kingdom everything that causes sin and all who do evil. They will throw them into the fiery furnace, where there will be weeping and gnashing of teeth. Then the righteous will shine like the sun in the kingdom of their Father."
>
> MATTHEW 13:40–43

In the meantime, we may not be able to change last year's harvest, but if we sow the right seeds, we can change *next year's* harvest. We can practice those disciplines that will strengthen our relationship with the Father. We sow to the Spirit when we choose to make God the motivating influence in our lives and worshipping Him the passion of our hearts. We sow to the Spirit when we read the Bible and meet with God's people. We sow to the Spirit when we are wholly submissive to God's will for our lives.

When we turn from the flesh and run back into His waiting arms, we can be thankful our Father never turns away His errant children.

Chapter Five

RECONCILING WITH THOSE YOU'VE HURT

"God, you'll never get me!"

Those were the words of a Christian man who was told by a counselor that he should humble himself and ask his children to forgive him for his hot temper and years of harsh, inconsistent discipline. At first the man resisted the idea, arguing that he would be showing weakness. "Men— real men—just don't do those things!" he protested. Nevertheless, God eventually did "get" him. Even the man's oldest son, his most rebellious child, embraced his weeping father when they reconciled.

That's the power of loving, humble confession!

Sin always divides; grace always unites.

Everyone who has received God's forgiveness should be highly motivated to reconcile with those he or she has wronged. The search for reconciliation lies at the heart of who God is, and those who have been reconciled to Him should seek to be reconciled to others. In fact, it is not possible to be in true fellowship with God without wanting to be in fellowship with others. The deeper the work of God in the human heart, the deeper our desire for reconciliation.

After all, as children of God, we belong to a family. If you are out of sorts with someone to whom you are unrelated, that's nearly always less upsetting than if there are irreconcilable differences within your family. As brothers and sisters in Christ, there are few things so deserving of our tears as when the family of God is torn by strife and simmering bitterness.

In one church, there were two brothers who had not spoken to each other for twenty years because of a petty disagreement. They would even enter and exit through separate doorways! Finally, one of the men approached the other to ask for his forgiveness. The pastor brought the two men to the church basement where the deacons prayed for them during a counseling session. The ordeal was difficult, but the forgiveness was genuine. The next Sunday the two men sang a duet together. They then told their story to the packed church, and God used this time to begin a spiritual renewal throughout the whole congregation. Eventually, a domino effect spread this revival to other churches in the area.

Sometimes asking for forgiveness brings unexpected results.

A man divorced his wife and married the woman with whom he had committed adultery. Years later, after he and his new wife had several children together, he learned he was suffering from terminal cancer. The reality of his impending death encouraged the man to do what should have happened long ago: He asked his ex-wife to forgive him for his sin against God and against her. As for his present wife, she was not able to care for their children because of a growing mental condition. So this woman—the ex-wife—not only forgave her adulterous ex-husband, but also adopted his children and loved them as if they were her own! She said, "I accept them as a gift from God…and receive them as Jesus has received me."

That's the power of forgiveness.

Paul said, "I strive always to keep my conscience clear before God and man" (Acts 24:16). You and I should be able to look anyone in the eye and know that we have done all within our power to be reconciled with that person. A clear conscience is a most precious treasure that we should seek, no matter the cost. The truly committed Christian knows he cannot have uninterrupted fellowship with God if he has not made every effort to have uninterrupted fellowship with his fellow man.

But after we've blown it, to whom do we owe an apology? What do we say? And what do we do when we fail?

THE BALL IS IN YOUR COURT

We must take the initiative to confess our failures to those we have wronged. Suppose there is a rift between you and someone else and you are quite convinced that you are 20 percent to blame, while in your opinion the other person is responsible for 80 percent of the problem. Your natural inclination is to think that *the other party* should come to *you* to repair the relationship. But let me say this clearly: *You must treat your 20 percent as if it is the full 100 percent.* You are responsible for your part of the rift, however big or small.

Possibly your confession will be the bridge over which the other individual will cross and in turn ask forgiveness from you. Often our efforts to make things right touches others in their spirit, prompting them to do the same. But—and this is important—we must be willing to take the first step, whatever the response of the other person. We must clear up our side of the ledger without implicating our offender. We must treat our smaller part as if it were the *whole* of the problem; then we must simply commit the other person to God and not take his or her responsibility upon ourselves.

And when we confess our wrong, we should not use that little word *if.* Don't say, *"If* I have hurt you…" Let's not pretend that we could be wrong about the situation when we know our guilt all too well. Rather, we should simply say, "I have offended you, and I have come to ask your forgiveness." Then we must specify our offense so there is no doubt about the issue being resolved. Then we add, "I hope you find it in your heart to forgive me."

What we'd like to hear is, "Yes, I do forgive you." But most people will avoid saying those words, not wanting to make a clear statement of forgiveness. More likely, they will say, "It's no big deal." But we should not be satisfied. Pause and say, "Well, to me it is a big deal. I really do need to hear you say the words, 'I forgive you.'"

Remember, sometimes people will be reluctant to extend forgiveness, because when they clear your record, they are left with the unpleasant task of taking care of their side of the ledger. It's like removing the weight from your side of a teeter-totter—now they are left to face their own part of the offense.

If the person says, "I don't know if I can forgive you," ask him to let you know when he is ready. And if he does not forgive you, at least you know that you have done what you could to take care of your part of the offense. In that knowledge, your conscience can rest.

TO WHOM IT MAY CONCERN

Our confession must be as broad as the offense. In most instances, if you have wronged or offended one person, you must go only to that person. If you have stolen money from the church, you should confess your sin to the church leadership. If you have embezzled funds, you must confess to those whom you have wronged, no matter how large the circle.

Does a man who has committed adultery need to confess that sin to his wife? Yes, I believe that he does, as does the wife who has cheated on her husband. Given the nature of the marriage bond, immorality is a sin both against the person *with* whom it is committed and *against* the spouse whose trust has been violated. It is best to make such confessions with the help of a pastor or counselor.

For the most part, we don't need to confess our thoughts to one another. If I am angry with you and you don't know it, it isn't necessary for me to confess my anger to you. A man who lusts after another woman should never, under any circumstances, confess his sinful thoughts to her, for that may only awaken greater desires in both of them. Sins of the mind are almost always best left with God.

Should we confess offenses we committed long ago? Let me ask, how long does it take you to forget that a friend cheated you out of, say, five thousand dollars? A year? Ten years? How long will you remember the time when someone you loved lied to you? Without forgiveness and reconciliation, we will take such memories to the grave. Very seldom does time obscure the memory of a bad deed. Only forgiveness can cause us to forget.

A woman asked me, "Should I confess to having lied under oath twenty-five years ago?" Lying under oath is a serious offense; indeed, God says that hell is filled with liars. And yet, now that twenty-five years have passed, the circumstances have likely changed quite drastically, so it might not be feasible for her to "confess" to all the people involved. Confession to someone else might be helpful, but sometimes we just have to pray to God and ask for wisdom on how to resolve these situations.

COUNTING THE COST

Finally—and now it gets difficult—reconciliation may involve restitution (see Luke 19:8). When the Holy Spirit begins to convict us of our offenses, reconciliation may prove costly.

A contractor told me that for years he had been building houses with inferior materials. He had made a practice of promising a higher level of quality than he actually delivered to his customers. Now, suddenly, God was shining a light on his soul. Imagine the man's predicament. He was faced with a difficult question: *Am I willing to do whatever God requires of me, no matter the cost?*

With a growing desire to please God, the contractor took all of his savings, mortgaged his house, and paid back as much as he could to each of his customers. I asked him, "Was it worth it?" He replied, "It was worth every penny!"

What about the man who lied on an application for worker's compensation, saying that he was injured on the job when, in point of fact, the injury occurred while he was hunting? Every month—now and for the rest of his life—he is fraudulently receiving a check. When told that he should correct this, he replied, "Do you think I'd be so stupid as to tell the truth and go to jail, rather than simply accepting what happened and move on?" But how can you move on when you are continuing to receive funds based on deceit? Would it not be better to spend your days in prison with a clear conscience than in retirement knowing that each day you are displeasing God?

For one man, reconciliation in fact meant a life sentence in jail. As a teenager back in 1975, John Claypool committed a murder just "to see what it was like to kill someone." Though he had been a suspect, he was not convicted of the crime. When he later married and had children, he knew he would carry his secret to the grave.

But then John accepted Christ as his Savior and he knew what he had to do. In 1997, twenty-two years after the murder, John Claypool gave himself up to the authorities and was sent to prison. He later said:

> Yet God was faithful to His promise to uphold me. At the moment of truth, though I now was a prisoner of the law, I was set free before God for the first time in my life. I cannot describe the feeling of that burden completely lifted—the Lord now held His once disobedient child in His loving arms; and true to His promise, He did not let me fall! A wonderful peace came over my soul such as I had never known before. I am now confined to a maximum-security prison, serving time for second-degree murder. But I am more free and more at peace than at any other time in my life.[8]

A friend of mine admitted to me that he had falsified papers to become a citizen of the United States. "If I go to the authorities," he said, "I will be jailed then deported back to my country, where I will face reprisals."

What should he do?

Such questions can only be answered by another question: How desperately do you want to have a conscience that is as clear as the blue sky?

If you will choose a glorious eternity with Christ, you can know the peace you seek right now. But that does not mean that your life on earth will be without difficulty. Jesus taught that hardship and, for some, even death lie in the path of those who follow Him with a whole heart. Remember Dietrich Bonhoeffer's words: "When Christ calls a man, he bids him come and die."[9] We are to give up everything to follow Him.

We are never more like God than when we forgive; we are never more like humans than when we realize our need for forgiveness. Today I encourage you to take the steps needed to bring peace to any relationship where there is animosity and strife. Sometimes doing what is hard is to do what is best.

But what do we do if others won't forgive us?

Keep reading.

Chapter Six

WHEN SOMEONE
WON'T FORGIVE
YOU

A football coach was asked by his estranged wife to pick up their two-year-old daughter from a friend's house. Once in the car, the little girl fell asleep while her father ran a series of quick errands. Then he drove off to football practice, forgetting that his daughter was asleep in the back seat. When he returned two hours later, to his everlasting horror he discovered her body, lying dead in the intense heat of the car on an August afternoon.

He did not ask his ex-wife's forgiveness. She already hated him for other reasons; there was little use asking forgiveness, knowing he would be rebuffed. What is more, he believed that to ask for forgiveness would trivialize the dreadfulness of what had happened. For a precious daughter to die in an accident is one thing, but to have her suffocate because of his thoughtlessness was an offense for which he believed there could be no forgiveness or reconciliation.

What do we do when others won't forgive us?

As I have said, we must be willing to do our part, to take the initiative in the reconciliation process. We have to let our apology be known, even when we know it will be rebuffed. But there are times when a broken relationship cannot be mended. For instance, the man in prison who wrote to me saying that he had raped four women, leaving their lives in ruin. He had since received God's forgiveness, but he would have to live with the knowledge that he has destroyed four lives he probably cannot help repair.

Thankfully, in most cases we can take steps to bring at least some degree of healing to a ruptured relationship, even when reconciliation seems out of the question. Once we have done all within our power to mend the relationship, we must move on in our journey. We must remember that we have a date with destiny. Our struggle to connect with others gives us an opportunity to grow in the likeness of

Jesus, who didn't feel the need to resolve all of the issues of injustice that surrounded Him, but instead committed His case to the Highest Court (see 1 Peter 2:21–23). His Father, He knew, would eventually weigh everything on His scale.

AN ETERNAL PERSPECTIVE

So what do we do when we are at fault and others won't forgive us? What do we do if our apologies are interpreted as hollow expressions of self-seeking, guilt-relieving clichés? What do we do if a relationship simply cannot be repaired because of our past failures?

First, we must never give up hope, but constantly pray for God's blessing on the lives of those from whom we are estranged. Two missionaries who did not see eye to eye while serving together in South America eventually parted ways. With mistrust on both sides and each convinced of the rightness of their cause, a genuine reconciliation appeared beyond reach. But time and prayer often heal wounds and give us needed perspective. Today, the two missionaries have not only forgiven one another but are close friends.

Second, when our apologies have been rebuffed, when possible we must say to the person we have wronged, "I know you cannot forgive me now, but tell me when you might be able to. It would mean a lot to me if the time came when you could forgive me."

Third, we must simply transfer the entire matter to the shoulders of Jesus Christ. He can bear what we cannot. Let your sorrow over the broken relationship remind you of your great need for God's grace, but do not become paralyzed, thinking that life has come to an end. Jesus was not a failure because He didn't reconcile all people to Himself.

Two Christian men decided to purchase and renovate an old beach-front house and later resell it to make a profit. One of the men bought the house and the other, who did the renovations, put thousands of dollars on his personal credit card to purchase material and supplies. Of course, he expected to be reimbursed for these expenses. But after the house was renovated, it simply would not sell. The man with the high credit card debt insisted that he be reimbursed for the cost of the materials, while the man who financed the purchase of the house argued that he had no money and could only repay his friend when the house sold.

The men could not be reconciled on this issue. They had genuine differences regarding how the matter should be resolved. Even with the best of intentions, relationships are often left hanging with loose ends. When we have done all we can, we must believe that God will resolve these matters in His own way, perhaps in this life but most assuredly in the life to come.

Sometimes we must accept the death of a relationship. We should know in our hearts that we have done everything possible to rectify our failures, but in our fallen world we will not always be successful. The woman whose child died in the car will probably never forgive her negligent husband. The rape victims will likely never grant the perpetrator forgiveness, even if he should ask for it.

We must therefore take comfort in the knowledge that God will eventually bring all things into the light:

> Therefore judge nothing before the appointed time; wait till the Lord comes. He will bring to light what is hidden in darkness and will expose the motives of men's hearts.
>
> 1 CORINTHIANS 4:5

At the judgment seat of Christ, all unresolved matters between believers will be adjudicated. As for the unconverted, they will bear the full weight of their sin forever. Thus, in either case, justice shall be done. Punishment will be administered according to the most meticulous standards. We will forever sing of God's true and righteous judgments.

It is true that, in human courts, "justice delayed is justice denied." However, God never loses evidence. Nor does He contaminate his findings over a period of time. That's why we can wait until the final Day of judgment for His righteous resolution. When we have done all we can do to restore the relationship, we must separate ourselves from the urge to take matters into our own hands. Rather, we must defer our case to God, confident that all accounts will eventually be settled.

King David came to the end of his life still unable to reconcile with all those he had wronged. After murdering Uriah to cover up his adulterous liaison with Bathsheba, David asked for and received God's forgiveness. But his tears could not restore the purity of Bathsheba; nor could his remorse bring back the life of Uriah. David's other wives were angry at his favoritism toward Bathsheba after she moved into the palace. His sons generally despised him because of the hypocrisy of his moral failure.

Yet even as he knew that the mess he'd created would never be cleaned up, David rejoiced in God.

He prayed:

Let me hear joy and gladness;
    let the bones you have crushed rejoice.
Hide your face from my sins
    and blot out all my iniquity.

Create in me a pure heart, O God,
    and renew a steadfast spirit within me....
Restore to me the joy of your salvation
    and grant me a willing spirit, to sustain me.
Then I will teach transgressors your ways,
    and sinners will turn back to you.

PSALM 51:8–10, 12–13

Words of hope for all who have ever blown it!

The publisher and author would love to hear your
comments about this book. *Please contact us at:*
www.bigchangemoments.com

NOTES

1. Peter Johnson, "Greene, a 'Lost Voice,' Awaits Renewal," *USA Today,* March 5, 2003, D4.

2. Martin Luther, as told in C. F. W. Walther, *The Proper Distinction Between Law and Gospel* (St. Louis, MO: Concordia Publishing House, 1986), 108.

3. William G. Justice, *Guilt and Forgiveness* (Grand Rapids, MI: Baker Book House, 1980), 95.

4. Ibid., 105.

5. C. S. Lewis, *Letters of C. S. Lewis,* ed. W. H. Lewis (New York: Harcourt Brace Jovanovich, 1966), 230.

6. C. H. Spurgeon, "Grace Abounding," *The Spurgeon Archive,* www.spurgeon.org/sermons/0501.htm (accessed September 26, 2003). From a sermon delivered at the Metropolitan Tabernacle, Newington, on March 22, 1863.

7. Excerpted from *I Kissed Dating Goodbye* © 1997, 2003 by Joshua Harris. Used by permission of Multnomah Publishers, Inc.

8. John Claypool, told to Ken Hyatt, "Freedom Behind Bars," *The Standard,* April 1999, 22–23.

9. Dietrich Bonhoeffer, *The Cost of Discipleship* (New York: Simon & Schuster, 1995). First published in German in 1937.

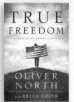

BIG CHANGE

AFTER YOU'VE BLOWN IT
Reconnecting with God and Others
ERWIN LUTZER ISBN 1-59052-334-2
(Available March 2004)

Do you feel like God will never take you back? Would you like a new beginning in your relationships? Award-winning author and pastor Erwin Lutzer offers practical help toward reconciliation.

THE PURITY PRINCIPLE
God's Safeguards for Life's Dangerous Trails
RANDY ALCORN ISBN 1-59052-195-1

God has placed warning signs and guardrails to keep us from plunging off the cliff. Find straight talk about sexual purity in Randy Alcorn's one-stop handbook for you, your family, and your church.

THE GRACE AND TRUTH PARADOX
Responding with Christlike Balance
RANDY ALCORN ISBN 1-59052-065-3

Living like Christ is a lot to ask! Discover Randy Alcorn's two-point checklist for Christlikeness—and begin to measure everything by the simple test of grace and truth.

A LITTLE POT OF OIL
A Life Overflowing
JILL BRISCOE ISBN 1-59052-234-6

What if He's asking you to pour out more than you can give? Step into the forward motion of God's love—and find the power of the Holy Spirit!

SMALL BOOKS
BIG CHANGE

www . b i g c h a n g e m o m e n t s . c o m

BIG CHANGE

PRESSURE PROOF YOUR MARRIAGE
Family First Series, #3
DENNIS & BARBARA RAINEY ISBN 1-59052-211-7

Dennis and Barbara Rainey show you how to use pressure to your benefit, building intimacy with each other and with the Lord.

WRESTLING WITH GOD
Prayer That Never Gives Up
GREG LAURIE ISBN 1-59052-044-0

You struggle with God in your own unique way. See how your struggle can result in the most rewarding relationship with Him!

IN THE SECRET PLACE
For God and You Alone
J. OTIS LEDBETTER ISBN 1-59052-252-4

Receive answers to some of life's most perplexing questions—and find deeper fellowship alone in the place where God dwells.

OUR JEALOUS GOD
Love That Won't Let Me Go
BILL GOTHARD ISBN 1-59052-225-7

God's intense jealousy for you is your highest honor, an overflowing of sheer grace. And when you understand it better, it becomes a pathway to countless blessings.

BIG CHANGE

GOD IS UP TO SOMETHING GREAT
Turning Your Yesterdays into Better Tomorrows
TONY EVANS ISBN 1-59052-038-6

THE HEART OF A TENDER WARRIOR
Becoming a Man of Purpose
STU WEBER ISBN 1-59052-039-4

SIMPLY JESUS
Experiencing the One Your Heart Longs For
JOSEPH M. STOWELL ISBN 1-57673-856-6

SIX STEPS TO SPIRITUAL REVIVAL
God's Awesome Power in Your Life
PAT ROBERTSON ISBN 1-59052-055-6

CERTAIN PEACE IN UNCERTAIN TIMES
Embracing Prayer in an Anxious Age
SHIRLEY DOBSON ISBN 1-57673-937-6

THE CROSS CENTERED LIFE
Experiencing the Power of the Gospel
C. J. MAHANEY ISBN 1-59052-045-9

THE DANGEROUS DUTY OF DELIGHT
The Glorified God and the Satisfied Soul
JOHN PIPER ISBN 1-57673-883-3

RIGHT WITH GOD
Loving Instruction from the Father's Heart
RON MEHL ISBN 1-59052-186-2

A PRAYER THAT MOVES HEAVEN
RON MEHL ISBN 1-57673-885-X

THE LOTUS AND THE CROSS
Jesus Talks with Buddha
RAVI ZACHARIAS ISBN 1-57673-854-X

SENSE AND SENSUALITY
Jesus Talks with Oscar Wilde
RAVI ZACHARIAS ISBN 1-59052-014-9

THE TREASURE PRINCIPLE
Discovering the Secret of Joyful Giving
RANDY ALCORN ISBN 1-57673-780-2
THE TREASURE PRINCIPLE BIBLE STUDY
ISBN 1-59052-187-0

GROWING A SPIRITUALLY STRONG FAMILY
Family First Series, #1
DENNIS & BARBARA RAINEY
ISBN 1-57673-778-0

TWO HEARTS PRAYING AS ONE
Family First Series, #2
DENNIS & BARBARA RAINEY
ISBN 1-59052-035-1

THE POWER OF CRYING OUT
When Prayer Becomes Mighty
BILL GOTHARD ISBN 1-59052-037-8

SMALL BOOKS
BIG CHANGE

www.bigchangemoments.com